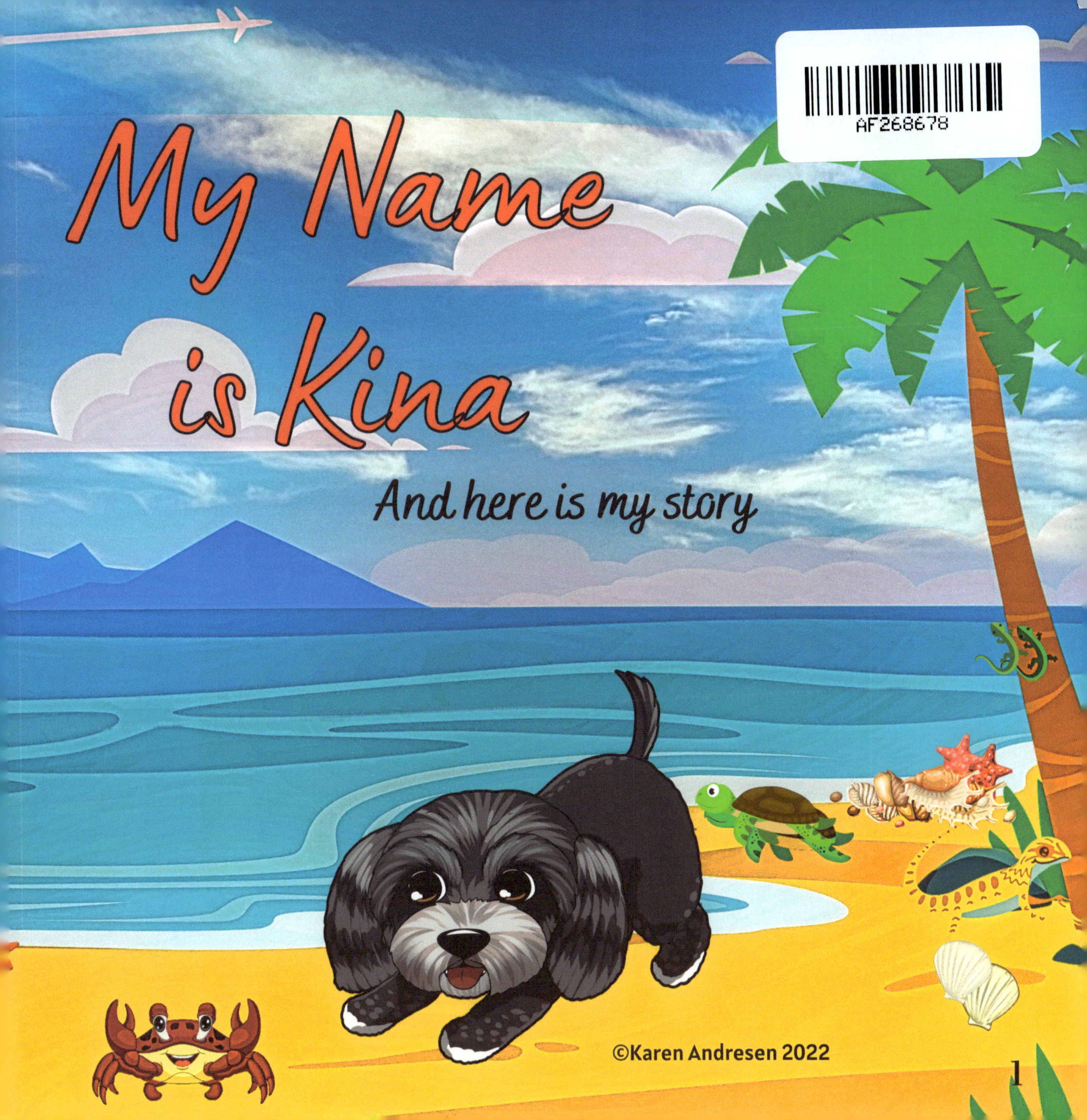

My Name
is Kina
And here is my story
©Karen Andresen 2022
1

One day when I was very little, my brother and I were dumped at a construction site. It was the worst day of our lives! We were so scared!

The first night was full of terror, and soon we became hungry. My brother wouldn't stop crying.

3

Then one day, this man appeared. He looked frightening, and my brother and I tried to hide from him.

The man took us to his home. This place was full of other dogs, and it was very noisy there, but the man was so kind to us.

The man's name was Juan, and he gave me my name. I thought Kina was as good a name as any. He called my brother, Kino.

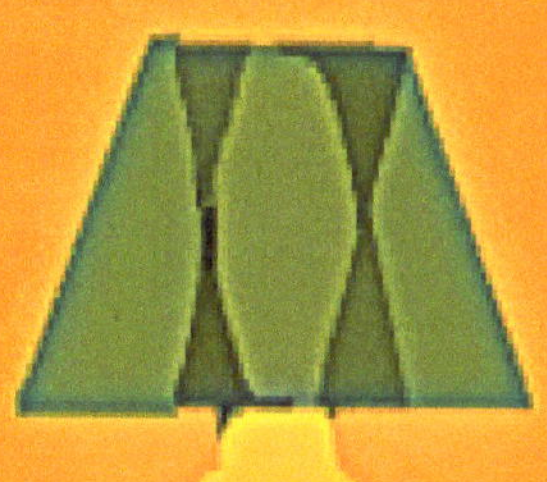

We settled into life in our new home, but it was often hectic and noisy. I wouldn't say I liked it very much, but Juan loved us. We would all take turns sleeping in his bed. I was happy to be loved like that.

Maybe this wasn't my perfect forever home, but I was happy because we were safe and we had food.
MEX
But one day, everything changed. Once again, we were scooped up and taken on a long journey.
8

After travelling a long time, we arrived at a new home with a new person and other dogs we did not know. Even though the lady was kind, I was miserable and Kino wouldn't stop crying!

Within weeks, Kino and I were moved to yet another house. I was beginning to resign myself to the fact that this was my life. All I wanted was a forever home. I was so sad that I didn't even want to eat anything.

Then, one day this lady came to see us. I had never seen her before, but she seemed very nice. I guess she thought I should be eating more because she said I was too skinny. So, she took me to her house. I was very excited!

I slowly inspected the place and thought, wait, is this my new home? I was overjoyed, and suddenly I was hungry. Then, a bowl of food appeared.
Maybe this is my new home!!

After that, the nice lady took me back to the noisy place where my brother was. I felt abandoned once again. I couldn't help but think that I would never find my forever home.
I felt very depressed.

The next day, I felt even sadder, and when the nice lady came back, I barely lifted my head to look at her.

14

For some reason, the nice lady scooped me up and seemed quite concerned. Then, she proceeded to look me over and carry me down the street like there was something wrong with me. Didn't she understand that she broke my heart??

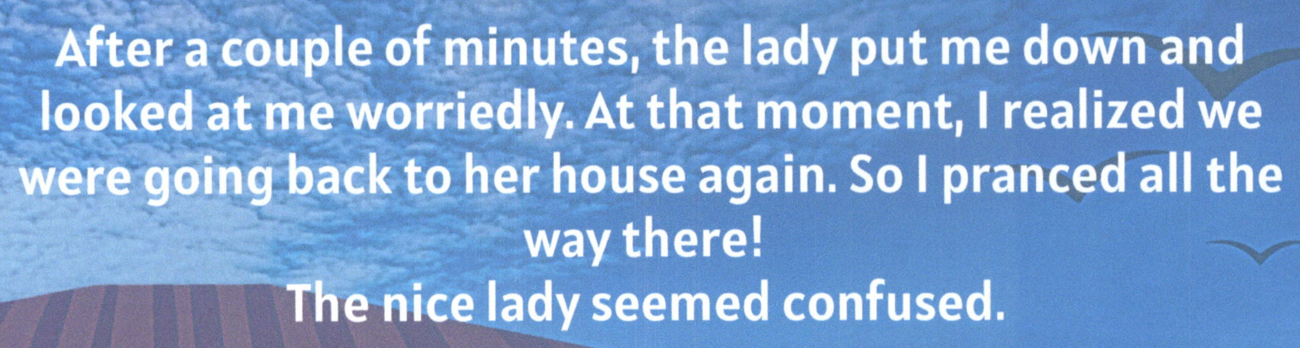
After a couple of minutes, the lady put me down and looked at me worriedly. At that moment, I realized we were going back to her house again. So I pranced all the way there!
The nice lady seemed confused.

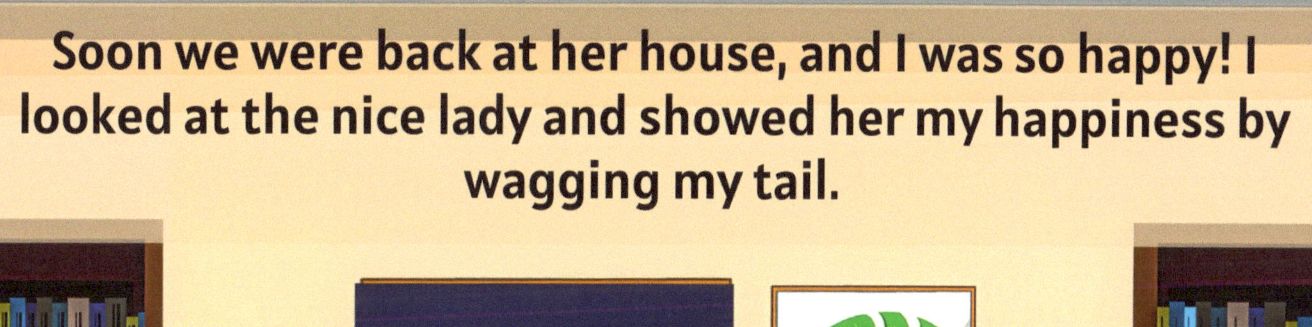

Soon we were back at her house, and I was so happy! I looked at the nice lady and showed her my happiness by wagging my tail.

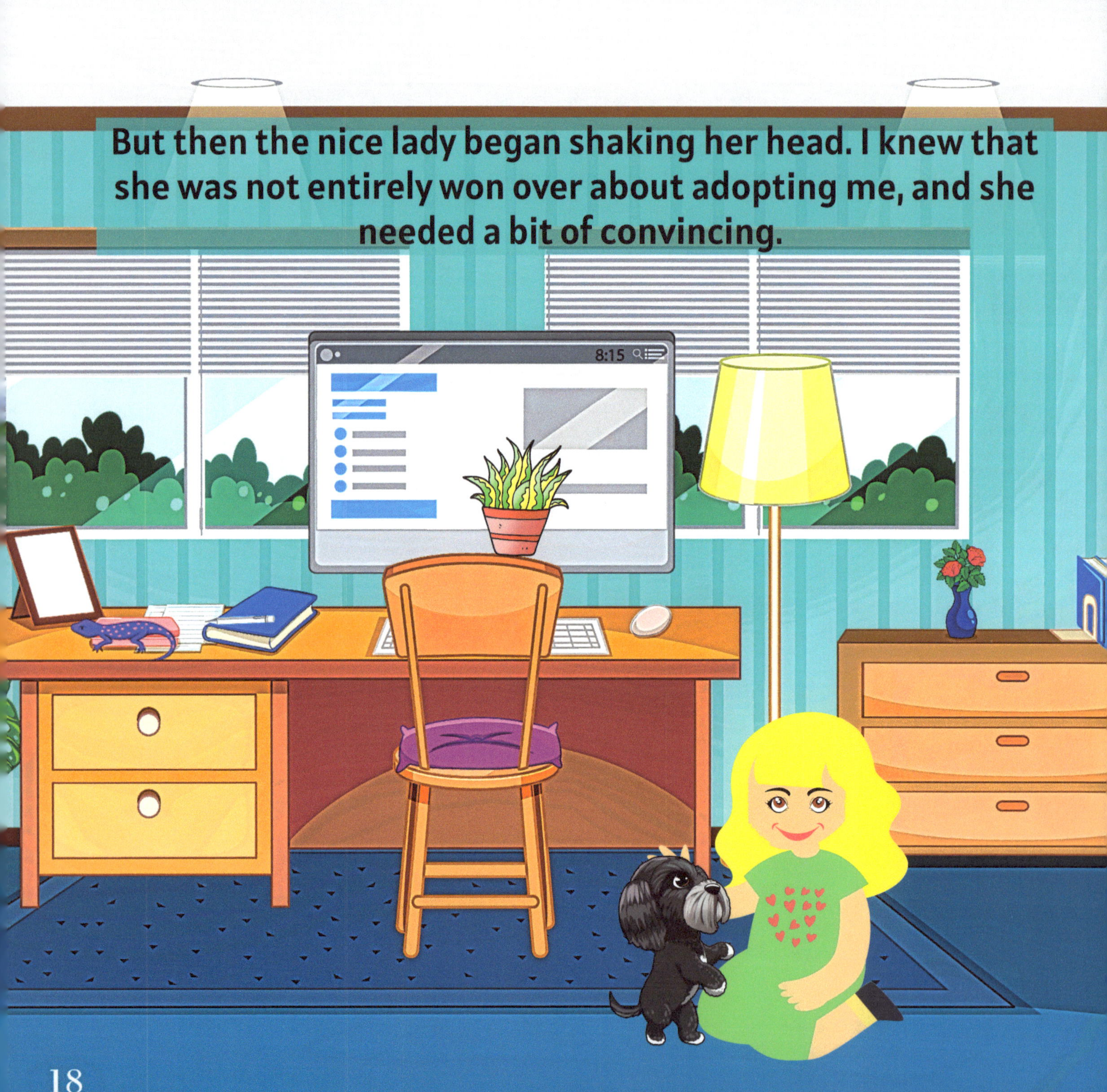

But then the nice lady began shaking her head. I knew that she was not entirely won over about adopting me, and she needed a bit of convincing.

That was when the nice lady started to get scared as she stared down at me. I tried asking her, "you're keeping me right? This is my forever home, right?"
I was so overjoyed that I just wanted to do a happy dance!

But she kept saying things like, "No, no, no, I can't have a dog! I don't have much money. I don't have a house or a stable life!!"
I tried to tell her that it would be okay as long as we were together.
You got this!
20

The poor nice lady looked terribly distressed, and I did my best to reassure her. I told her,
" I can go with you when you move to another house, I will eat anything you give me and when you go to a restaurant, I will crawl under the table and you will never know that I am there!"

The truth was, I loved her already. All I needed to do was make her love me.

Later, she took me to her friend's house. I think she hoped that they would tell her what a bad idea it was to adopt me.

But her friends could see that we were meant to be together. So they offered their support.

That day, I found out that the nice lady's name was Karen.

She still seemed a little scared, so it was my job to reassure her that everything would be all right. But, to be honest, I think Karen needed someone to take care of her more than I did.

That night, she told me that things would not always be easy, but we were going to be together forever. I felt pure happiness!

She never brought me back to the noisy house again, and later I heard that my brother had gone to a nice home in Canada. Sometimes dreams do come true!

Life with Karen is fun. I get to sleep in her bed and she takes me places. I even get to stay in nice hotels and ride on airplanes.

Of course, I take care of her too because she needs that.
So when she got really sick, I never left her side.
Kina says, "Thank you Dr Belloso for saving Karen."

I was happy when she got better, and we could resume our adventures together. ❤
We are the perfect match and we love each other very much.
Stay tuned for more Kina and Karen adventures!

About the Author

Karen and Kina currently live in Mexico, where Kina was adopted. Karen spends her days writing, teaching and hanging out with Kina, her best friend.

This book is dedicated in memory of Kina's rescuer, *Juan Ramon Velazquez Martinez.*
Also, a special thanks to Robin and No Borders Animal Rescue (NOBARS).

A REMINDER FROM KINA:
Please support your local animal shelter.